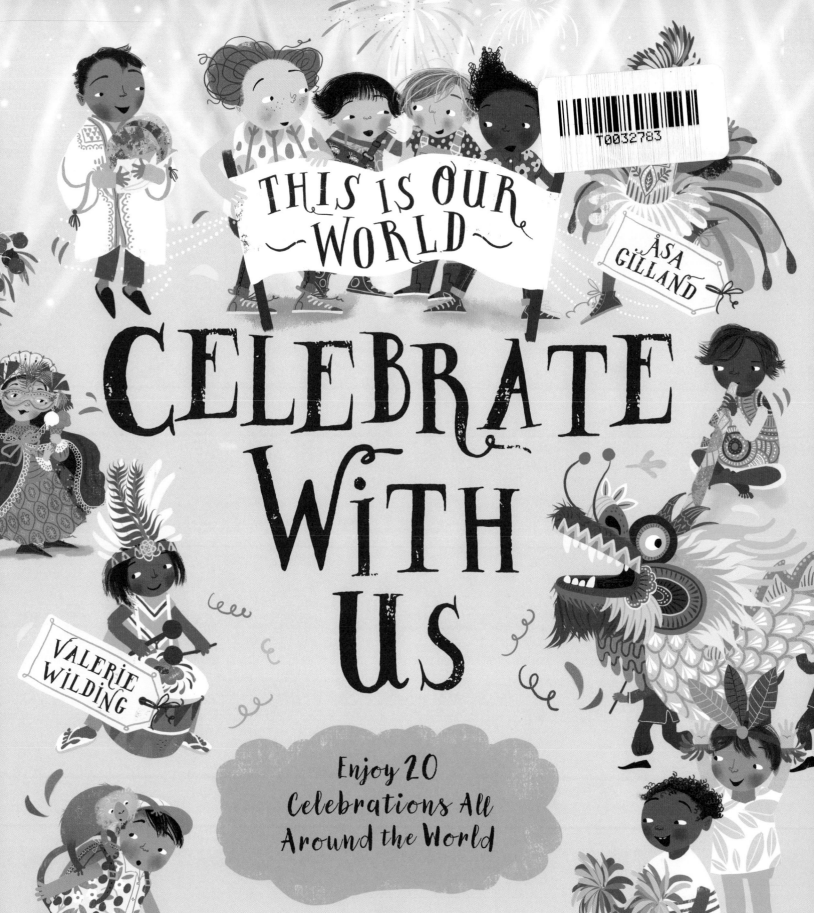

THIS IS OUR WORLD

CELEBRATE WITH US

ÅSA GILLAND

VALERIE WILDING

Enjoy 20
Celebrations All
Around the World

KINGFISHER
LONDON & NEW YORK

For Sue Watkinson, who loves a celebration—V.W.
To Ludvig, thank you for making every
celebration so special—Å.G.

Thank you to . . .
. . . Magdalena Jackson, Alkistis Pourtsidou, Philip Nierop, Emma Timmerman,
Joanna Butler, and Tim Gauntlett. And also to Melonie Matthews,
co-director of Gathering of Nations Ltd.

A Raspberry Book
Author: Valerie Wilding
Illustrator: Åsa Gilland
Editorial: Nicola Edwards and Tracey Turner
Art direction and cover design: Sidonie Beresford-Browne
Design: Nicky Scott

KINGFISHER
LONDON & NEW YORK

Distributed in the U.S. and Canada by Macmillan,
120 Broadway, New York, NY 10271

EU representative: Macmillan Publishers Ireland Ltd, 1st Floor, The Liffey Trust Centre,
117-126 Sheriff Street Upper, Dublin 1, D01 YC43

Library of Congress Cataloging-in-Publication Data has been applied for.

ISBN 978-0-7534-7850-9

Kingfisher books are available for special promotions and premiums.
For details contact: Special Markets Department, Macmillan, 120 Broadway,
New York, NY 10271

For more information, please visit
www.kingfisherbooks.com

Printed in China
9 8 7 6 5 4 3 2 1
1TR/0123/WKT/RV/128MA

FSC
www.fsc.org
MIX
Paper | Supporting
responsible forestry
FSC® C116313

CONTENTS

INTRODUCTION

All over the world and all through the year, people are always celebrating something special. Some festivals, like New Year, are celebrated in many countries, but not always on the same day. Others are unique to just one place, like the country that turns orange on the king's birthday!

Many of these special celebrations are central to different religions, and the same ones can be observed in similar ways in different parts of the world. Some help us remember events in the past. The natural world is celebrated, too, from the beauty of blossoms to a horde of hungry monkeys! All these celebrations give us a chance to create fresh memories.

Lots of celebrations feature street parades, and many of them involve months of work to make them so colorful and thrilling. In this book you'll find one parade that doesn't need a street, and one with dancing skeletons.

We learn about other people by visiting their festivals and sharing their traditions and culture. In this book there are 20 celebrations from around the world, and you're invited to all of them. Celebrations can be serious, exciting, or just plain fun. We look forward all year to these special days, and especially to sharing good times with family and friends.

So turn the pages and come celebrate!

GATHERING OF NATIONS, U.S.A.

ROSH HASHANAH, U.S.A.

EID AL-FITR, ENGLAND

KING'S DAY, NETHERLANDS

BASTILLE DAY, FRANCE

LAS FALLAS, SPAIN

THE DAY OF THE DEAD, MEXICO

INTERNATIONAL FESTIVAL OF THE SAHARA, TUNISIA

CARNIVAL IN RIO, BRAZIL

A WORLD of CELEBRATIONS

MARTIN'S DAY, GERMANY

CHRISTMAS EVE, POLAND

NEW YEAR'S EVE, UKRAINE

CARNIVAL OF VENICE, ITALY

EASTER, GREECE

DIWALI, INDIA

MID-AUTUMN FESTIVAL, CHINA

LUNAR NEW YEAR, KOREA

CHERRY BLOSSOM FESTIVAL, JAPAN

MONKEY BUFFET FESTIVAL, THAILAND

BARUNGA FESTIVAL, AUSTRALIA

BARUNGA FESTIVAL

I'm Kirra, from the Bagala clan of the Jawoyn people.
Our ancestors have lived in Australia for over 60,000 years!

Every June, people from all over the world visit our community of Barunga, where we have a really fun festival. It's exciting to see the population of Barunga grow to ten times its normal size for one weekend. We don't have hotels, so most visitors camp.

The Barunga Festival celebrates the history and traditions of the Aboriginal peoples of Australia, and the Torres Strait Islanders, who live north of Queensland.

The Barunga Festival is celebrated on a 3-day holiday weekend every June in Barunga, in Australia's Northern Territory.

DIDGERIDOO

DRIED PANDANUS LEAVES

There are always lots of workshops and activities. My aunt shows visitors how she weaves baskets from dried pandanus leaves.

This year I'm going to do a spear-making workshop, and my brother's doing a musical instrument workshop with our dad. They're going to make a didgeridoo using a tree branch that's been hollowed out by insects called termites.

Visitors can watch soccer, basketball, and softball games all weekend if they like. There's plenty of traditional music and dancing, too, and crafts to buy and "bush tucker" stalls. Bush tucker is any food that's native to Australia, like nuts, seeds, fruits, honey, and different meats.

I'm a Barunga Junior Guide. We take visitors on bush walks and show them stuff like how to eat quandong and rosella flowers and the seeds you find inside.

Barunga has no electricity, so many campers buy food in our store and cook dinner over a fire. (They have to bring their own firewood!) Sometimes we make friends with visiting kids and we get invited to join their campfire. I love evenings around a fire, singing or listening to music and watching flying foxes with their big bat wings spread either side of their foxy faces.

QUANDONG

ROSELLA FLOWERS

JUNIOR GUIDE

FLYING FOX

LAS FALLAS

Hola! I am Mateo. In Valencia, Spain, where I live, we have the best (and noisiest) festival. It's called Las Fallas—our Festival of Fire—and it happens every March.

Las Fallas celebrates the coming of spring and St. Joseph the carpenter, who is the patron saint of craftsmen. In the old days, carpenters in Valencia stood their candles on wooden planks to give them light to work by. Once spring came, they didn't need the candles, so they burned the planks. Valencia has a special way of commemorating this old tradition.

For two weeks, firecrackers explode every day at two o'clock, but after that the festival really gets going! There are daily parades with marching bands and people in traditional costumes.

VALENCIAN COSTUMES

For months, people have been busy creating **ninots**, which are giant statues made of wood, cardboard, and papier-mâché. They're carefully piled together in stacks called **fallas**, which are sometimes almost 65 feet (20 meters) high.

NINOTS

Fallas appear all over the city, and many of the **ninots** are very funny. The judges come around the next day and award prizes for the best ones. Everyone in the children's home where I live enters a competition to see who can spot the most **ninots** of famous people.

On the last day, all those fantastic **ninots** are burned! Across the city, the sound of firecrackers signals the burning. All that work goes up in flames! But the **ninots** hide a secret: there are fireworks inside them, so as they burn, they burst into explosions and showers of sparks.

FALLAS MUSEUM

Each year one **ninot** is saved from burning and put in the Fallas Museum. It's the one that everyone voted the best of all!

CHERRY BLOSSOM FESTIVAL

My name is Keiko. I live in Osaka, Japan, with my mom, grandfather, and brother, Haruki. We have such a pretty festival! It's held to welcome the spring, and it's called *hanami*, which means "flower viewing." The flowers are sakura, the blossoms of the cherry tree.

This festival is celebrated in Japan every spring when the blossoms are at their best.

There are sakura trees all over Japan. Blossom time begins about the end of March, but each tree only blooms for a week or two. They remind us that our lives are short but precious.

Our park is full of sakura trees. When they bloom, they're like pink clouds. We spend the day beneath the trees, and my friend Hiroko comes with her family, too. At this time of year there's a daily blossom forecast so people know the best places for hanami. We set out early in the morning to get a good spot before the crowds come!

Some people wear traditional kimonos, but Hiroko, Haruki, and I wear comfy clothes. We have some snacks and play games. Then we love to lie back and admire the pink flowers against the blue sky and watch petals drifting down.

In the evening, we have our picnic! Haruki and Grandpa love little dumplings in different colors, called **hanami dango**. Everyone likes cherry blossom rice balls! Mom always brings **wagashi**, which are pretty sweets, and sakura-flavored cola drinks. Haruki's favorite chocolate bar is also sakura-flavored for hanami!

Hiroko and I like hanami best as it grows dark. Paper lanterns are strung between the trees, and they light up the blossoms. It's like a pink fairyland.

KIMONOS

HANAMI DANGO

WAGASHI

EASTER

Hello, I'm Christos, and I live in Greece. Easter is an important celebration for us because it's about Jesus rising from his tomb after he was crucified.

Easter is celebrated by Christians all over the world on different dates between March and April.

Just before Easter, my big sister Eleni and I make Easter biscuits, called **koulourakia**, then we make red eggs! Eleni cooks lots of eggs in vinegar, water, and red dye. When they're done, I shine them with a cloth and some oil. Mom takes some eggs to put inside the sweet **tsoureki** bread that she bakes.

KOULOURAKIA

SWEET TSOUREKI

On Easter Saturday evening, we take candles to church. We hear the Easter story, then the lights go out, and the priest goes and gets two lit candles. The flame is passed from candle to candle, and soon the church is bright. At midnight, the priest says, **"Christ is risen!"** and everyone hugs.

Outside there's a bonfire and fireworks. We get home very late and have a supper of **magiritsa**, our Easter lamb and vegetable soup.

We play a game with the red eggs called **tsougrisma**. You tap someone's egg with the pointy end of yours. If their egg cracks, you win, and you tap the next person's egg, and so on. The winning egg is the only one that doesn't break.

TSOUGRISMA

SWEET BAKLAVA

MAGIRITSA

Our aunt, uncle, and cousins come for Sunday lunch, and Eleni and I receive Easter gifts from our godparents. We eat roast lamb to honor Jesus, the lamb of God. We have lots of other dishes with it, and finish with our **koulourakia**, sweet baklava, and cheese with figs. Then the grown-ups fall asleep and we play!

BASTILLE DAY

Bonjour! I'm Lilou, and I live in Paris, France, where we have a special celebration on July 14. It's called La Fête Nationale, but many people know it as Bastille Day.

The Bastille was a grim fortress prison at a time when rich people ruled the country and the poor often didn't have enough to eat. Many people were desperate to change the way France was run.

On July 14, 1789, almost a thousand of them attacked the fortress. They broke in to steal the Bastille's supply of gunpowder and to free prisoners. It was the start of a revolution that got rid of the king and the wealthy nobles. France was changed forever.

Bastille Day is celebrated in France on July 14 every year.

On Bastille Day, my brother Jules and I get up early to go to the Avenue des Champs-Élysées and watch the military parade, which is fantastic!

Thousands of men and women from the army, navy, and air force march past us, and there are airplanes, helicopters, and tanks, too. I like the helicopters best! Marching bands play loud music, and there are firefighters and police and lots of horses, which Jules likes best.

In the afternoon, our uncle, aunt, and cousins come for a delicious lunch that lasts for hours. Papa sticks French flags on all the dishes! When it grows dark, we go to Uncle's office, which is high up. It has a perfect view of the tall Eiffel Tower, where there's an amazing firework display. While we watch, we drink hot chocolate and eat hot dogs in toasted brioche buns. It's the best part of the day!

BRIOCHE BUN

EID AL-FITR

Hello, I'm Maya, and I live in Yorkshire, in England. Every year we celebrate a happy Muslim festival called Eid al-Fitr. It means "Festival of Breaking the Fast." That's because Eid comes at the end of the holy month of Ramadan, which is when Muslims don't eat or drink between sunrise and sunset.

My little sister's much too young to fast. I'll start fasting when I'm about 12, Mom says. This year I'll practice a little by giving up candy, chocolate, and chips during Ramadan. Fasting reminds us of people who never have enough to eat. Muslims give to charity before Eid begins so everyone can celebrate with good food.

Ramadan's date changes every year, depending on when the new moon appears. Eid al-Fitr starts at the next new moon. We put up twinkly lights, and in the morning we hug, saying, "Eid Mubarak," which means "Blessed Eid." We give Eid cards and dress in new clothes.

After a small breakfast (big lunch later!) we go to the mosque for special Eid prayers. We thank Allah (God) for his goodness and for helping us to fast.

At home, we share a huge lunch with family and Mom's best friend, Inaya. We have biryani, samosas, pakoras, vegetable curry, salad, and more. Eid is known as "sweet Eid," so there are a lot of sweet things, too.

This festival is celebrated every year by Muslims all over the world, on different dates in spring or early summer.

EID MUBARAK!

After lunch, some of the adults give us presents. When we've eaten and our grandparents are resting, Mom takes us to tidy her grandparents' graves and say prayers for them. Then we go to the park to play with our friends and maybe make some new ones!

SAMOSAS

PAKORAS

BIRYANI

MARTIN'S DAY

I'm Emilia, and I live in Germany. Our town has a fun celebration called *Martinstag* (Martin's Day) every year. It's the special day of St. Martin of Tours.

Martin became a Christian when he was ten and grew up to be a soldier in the Roman army. One bitterly cold night, he was riding his horse through a snowstorm. He was very glad to have his army cloak. When he saw a beggar in rags, huddled on the frozen ground, Martin cut his cloak in two with his sword. He gave half to the beggar.

After Martin dreamed that Jesus was wearing half his cloak, he decided fighting was wrong. Just before a battle near Worms, in Germany, he announced that he wasn't going to fight. Instead he left the army to tell people about Jesus. One day the townspeople chose him to be their bishop, but Martin really wanted to continue the work he was doing. He hid in a barn with some geese, but they made such a racket that he was soon found. He did become a bishop!

At school we make paper lanterns and decorate them. We dangle the lanterns from sticks, and when it's dark we gather together in a procession. Everyone's thrilled to see St. Martin leading the way on a white horse. (Ssh, secret—it's my dad dressed up!) A band follows us, and we sing as we go.

Martin's Day is celebrated in Germany on November 11 every year. It's also celebrated in some other European countries and by German communities in the United States.

STUTENKERLE

In the town square, everyone stands around a bonfire eating **stutenkerle**. They're little baked people with currants for their eyes and buttons. We love them! Afterward we go home for a dinner of roast goose, and we remember St. Martin hiding in the barn.

Monkey Buffet Festival

I live in Thailand, and my name is Sunan. It's the last Sunday in November, and we're going to the Monkey Buffet Festival in Lopburi for the second time. My four brothers and I begged our parents to take us again because it's such fun!

The story of the monkey god, Hanuman, tells how he helped save Sita, the wife of Lord Rama, from a demon. Thai people respect monkeys because of this and believe they bring good fortune. The Lopburi people put out food for long-tailed macaque monkeys every day all year, but the festival is special.

This festival happens every November in Lopburi, Thailand.

Over the festival, about 4 tons of fruits and vegetables, cakes, soft drinks, bottles of water, and candies are set out for the monkeys. That's the same weight as an elephant!

It begins with a parade of men in monkey outfits and children in monkey masks. They walk to the ancient temple where the monkeys live.

There's even a row of monkey statues with food trays. Fruit is also arranged on the sides of a pyramid, or frozen in a block of ice. The monkeys love to lick that!

When they've eaten enough, the monkeys get mischievous! They leap onto people's backs and shoulders and pull their hair. I filmed a little monkey sitting on our dad's head. My brothers and I like feeding the small monkeys. They take the food so carefully with their paws.

Lopburi people love tourists visiting the festival. They say it's good for business, which is good for the monkeys because the people can afford to give them four fantastic feasts on festival day!

THE DAY OF THE DEAD

I'm Sofia, and I'm excited, because tomorrow we celebrate the Día de los Muertos, or Day of the Dead. We'll think of our loved ones who have died, and we believe that on this day they'll come and spend time among the living.

Every year we make an altar in our living room. My brother Diego and I put up pictures of our dead relatives. We add candles and orange marigold flowers, which we call **flores de muerto**—flowers of the dead. We hope the bright colors and scents will guide our loved ones to our home in Mexico City. Papá adds great-grandfather's favorite book and great-grandmother's music box.

FLORES DE MUERTO

Mamá makes **pan de muerto**, or "bread of the dead," and flavors it with orange. She molds lumps of dough into bone shapes to go on top, then sprinkles it with sugar. We're given little sugar skulls to eat, and Papá writes our names on them in icing.

PAN DE MUERTO

We go to the graveyard to clean the family headstones. Diego and I smother our relatives' graves with marigolds, and we take their favorite things to show that we still care for them. Then we light candles and sing and tell stories about the dead people. They're often very funny!

Later there's a huge street parade, thanks to James Bond. True! The movie **Spectre** starts with a Day of the Dead parade in Mexico City. Some important people thought, "What a great idea! Let's do it for real!" So now we have an exciting parade with music, singing, floats, fireworks, fancy costumes, and people with painted skeleton faces. It's **fantástico!**

The Day of the Dead takes place every year on November 1 and 2 in Mexico.

LUNAR NEW YEAR

Hi, I'm Joo-won. In Korea we love celebrating the Lunar New Year, which we call Seollal. It happens in January or February when there's a new moon. We celebrate for three days: on New Year's Day, on the day before, and the day after.

The new year is a time for families to be together, and our grandparents visit us for Seollal. On the first day we wear traditional clothes, called **hanbok**. I have a long jacket, called **jeogori**, and trousers, called **baji**. My twin sister Ji-woo wears a short **jeogori** and a bright pink wrap-around skirt, called a **chima**. She looks like a bell!

The Lunar New Year is celebrated in Korea (and other parts of the world) in January or February. Different countries have unique traditions.

JEOGORI

BAJI

CHIMA

Seollal's a time to think about family members who have died. We put offerings of food on a table and bow in a special way, called **sebae**, to honor our ancestors. Then we children perform **sebae** for the grown-ups and wish them good luck. Some of them give money to us afterward!

Our big Seollal feast always starts with special soup, called **tteokguk**. We put slices of rice cake in it, and the custom is that everyone who eats **tteokguk** at Seollal becomes one year older. The circles of rice cakes are shaped like coins, so we hope the soup will bring us good fortune.

TTEOKGUK

On New Year's Day we go to the amusement park. Ji-woo wants to go on everything, but I'm not crazy about fast rides. If the weather's right, I go kite flying with our cousins. We have kite fights!
I love Seollal!

27

CHRISTMAS EVE

Hello, I'm Magda, from Warsaw, Poland. We love Christmas! Every year we walk around the old town, gazing at thousands of Christmas lights. We drink hot chocolate and watch people ice skating.

On Christmas Eve we finish decorating our Christmas tree. I put the star on top and switch the lights on. It's beautiful! My sister looks through the window for the first star in the sky. When it appears, it's time for **Wigilia**, our special Christmas Eve supper.

Christmas is a Christian festival celebrating the birth of Christ on December 25. It's celebrated in different ways in many parts of the world.

When we sit at the table, my father always says, "Oh! I forgot the hay." He disappears for a while and comes back with wisps of hay, which he slips beneath the white tablecloth. The hay reminds us that Jesus was born in a manger.

OH! I FORGOT THE HAY.

OPLATEK

We set an extra place at our table in case someone unexpected comes by. We call it "the wanderer's place." It helps us remember Mary (the mother of Christ) and Joseph, who were desperate for somewhere to stay in Bethlehem.

SAUERKRAUT

Our feast begins with breaking a special wafer called **oplatek**. We share it with each other, saying, "Merry Christmas." Some families have twelve dishes of food, and some have thirteen. We have mushroom soup, salads, sauerkraut, and fish dishes, like fried carp and herring. My favorite sweet things are poppy seed cake and gingerbread. We're supposed to taste everything, but I pretend to try jellied carp. Fishy jelly doesn't sound good.

After supper, we find the tree has a heap of presents beneath it. Santa Claus visited while we were at *Wigilia*!

29

INTERNATIONAL FESTIVAL OF THE SAHARA

I'm Sami. I live in Douz, Tunisia, on the edge of the Sahara desert. Our festival lasts for four days. It started as the Camel Festival over 100 years ago, but it's grown a lot. Visitors come from all over the world to learn about the traditions and culture of North African desert people like me!

The opening ceremony starts with marching bands, followed by local people with camels, horses, and Sloughi dogs, which will soon be racing. Next come lots of dancers and musicians, especially drummers, in traditional costumes. It's very noisy!

There's so much for visitors to see and hear: poetry and songs, dancers in beautiful swirling costumes, and drummers dancing, too, twirling their drums as they bang them.

This festival is celebrated in Tunisia every December.

Everyone enjoys the horse races, especially me! I love the deafening sound of hoofbeats as they gallop past. Later the acrobatic horse riders perform. They turn upside down and backwards on a galloping horse. Some stand on the horse's back, swing down to the ground for a moment, then spring back into the saddle. A really skilled rider can grab a child and, next moment, they're both standing on the horse's back!

But my favorite event is sand hockey, which is very exciting! Sometimes you can't see the ball for the clouds of sand, and the players whack more sand into the air trying to hit it. My friends and I play after school—we call ourselves the Sand Devils. Maybe we'll play in the festival next year!

KHOBZ EL MELLA

Douz has a big market where you can buy local food, like **khobz el mella**. It's stuffed flatbread—a little like pizza with the topping on the inside. I always eat some on my way home. Scrumptious!

NEW YEAR'S EVE

Hello, I'm Oksana, and I live in Kyiv. New Year's Eve is very special for Ukrainians. We decorate a tree with tiny lights, sparkly ornaments, and a shining gold star. Our tree stays up until Christmas Day, which we celebrate on January 7.

The New Year is celebrated by most people in the world, though there are different calendars. New Year in the Gregorian calendar begins on January 1.

After lunch our parents take me and my brothers, Mykola, Illya, and Danilo, to the city square. A tall Christmas tree covered in golden lights stands in the middle, and everywhere is decorated for the holidays. It looks magical! There's a fair with rides, and stalls selling souvenirs and tasty things to eat.

PORTZELKY

KYIV CAKE

In the evening our aunts come for dinner, and we have plenty of delicious food. Mykola's favorite is fried raisin cookies called **portzelky**. Illya and I love *Kyiv cake* best. It has meringue and nuts inside and a chocolatey top!

Just before midnight, our president speaks on TV and wishes us "Z novym rokom" —Happy New Year. Little Danilo shouts the last ten seconds of the year, then we wish each other "Z novym rokom," too.

Z NOVYM ROKOM

Every year there's a spectacular firework display. We can watch it from our apartment balcony! Afterward, we wrap up warm and go outside to slide around in the snow with our friends and to wish our neighbors "Z novym rokom."

We fall asleep hoping that Grandfather Frost and his granddaughter, Snegurochka, the Snow Maiden, will leave some New Year presents under our tree. We've been good all year, so we're sure they will!

GRANDFATHER FROST

SNEGUROCHKA

CARNIVAL of VENICE

I'm Anna, and I live in a beautiful city of canals and bridges and alleys—Venice! For two weeks every year we have a wonderful carnival, when everything is decorated, especially the boats, including the famous Venetian gondolas.

People parade every day in gorgeous costumes and masks. Venice is famous for masks, and some of them are very fancy! No one can tell if the person they're talking to is rich or poor, or famous, like a rock star. Everyone's equal at Carnival.

Mamma, Papà, and I always decorate plain white masks. I use paint, feathers, gems, and sequins for mine! My costume has a beautiful long cape. It's poppy red, trimmed with cream-colored lace and gold ribbons. When we go out walking, no one recognizes me, so I pretend I'm a queen. Luckily, the mask only reaches to the end of my nose, so I can still eat ice cream!

Gondolas and other boats fill the Grand Canal, all decorated and lit with hundreds of lights. Some carry singers and dancers, even fire eaters and acrobats. A gondala transformed into a giant seagull made me laugh!

This celebration is held in Venice, Italy, every year in February or March.

Parties, balls, and magic shows happen all the time. There's ice skating, music, and dancing, too. We love the Best Costume and Best Mask competitions in the Piazza San Marco. While we watch, we eat **fritelle**. They're like little sugary doughnuts, stuffed with pine nuts and raisins, or with chocolate custard! Delicious!

FRITELLE

GATHERING of NATIONS

My name's Kimi, and my mom's from the Navajo tribe of American Indians, so my brother Kai and I are half Navajo. We live in Albuquerque, New Mexico, and we're lucky because a big powwow is held here every year. It's called the Gathering of Nations, and it's where American Indians from hundreds of tribes meet together to celebrate their culture.

One year I made friends with Nova, a girl from the Hopi tribe. We meet up at every Gathering now, and we message each other all the time. Last year she brought me a Hopi **kachina** doll and I gave her a Navajo turquoise friendship bracelet.

The Gathering of Nations is held every April in Albuquerque, New Mexico.

The Gathering lasts for three days, and over 100,000 people attend. For the opening ceremony, the performers wear traditional clothes and headdresses and enter the arena in a spiral until it's packed full. We can hardly hear ourselves speak over the sound of drums, dancing feet, and singing.

Three thousand dancers attend the Gathering, and there are 36 dance competitions. My favorite is the women's shawl dance. They wear brightly colored shawls with long fringes and dance to a drum beat, swirling their shawls like wings.

One thing we never miss is the Horse and Rider Regalia parade. The horses are dressed up almost as much as the riders!

Nova, Kai, and I like the Indian Traders' Market. There are stalls selling jewelry, clothes, moccasins, feathers, dream catchers, and all sorts of things. Last time, Mom bought Navajo turquoise earrings, Kai bought a pottery turtle, and I got a box with a turtle painted on it. Mom said turtles are an important symbol to most American Indian peoples, and they will keep us healthy and wise!

MOCCASINS

DIWALI

I'm Ravi, and I live in Ayodhya, India, with my two sisters, my mom, and my grandmother. Every October or November, just before the new moon, we celebrate Diwali, the Hindu Festival of Lights. Diwali honors Lakshmi, the goddess of good fortune, and it symbolizes the victory of goodness over evil and light over darkness.

The story of Diwali tells how Prince Rama's wife Sita was kidnapped by a demon. Sita was rescued by Rama, his brother Lakshman, and the monkey god Hanuman. They returned home at night and people lit lamps to welcome them. Other parts of Asia have different Diwali legends. In south India, for example, people celebrate the victory of Lord Krishna over the demon king Narakasura.

Before Diwali, we clean the house and set out little clay lamps, called diyas. Mom puts lights over our front door. My sisters and I use colored rice flour, petals, and chalk to make a pattern on the ground outside to tell Lakshmi and Rama and all our visitors that they are welcome in our home.

DIYAS

LAKSHMI

On Diwali, the **diyas** are lit, and we wear new clothes. We spend the day with family and friends and give them delicious sweets of different shapes, sizes, colors, and flavors. We pray to Lakshmi for good luck in the new year, which starts the next day.

At night, all the buildings are decorated with lights and flowers. But the most amazing sight is the river, where hundreds of thousands of lights line the banks. Sometimes there is a laser light show, too—we light our homes and lasers light the sky!

39

ROSH HASHANAH

Hi, I'm *Adam*, and I live in New York City. Our family is Jewish, and in the fall we celebrate our New Year, Rosh Hashanah, which means "head of the year." We wish people a sweet and good year, and we hope we'll have one, too.

We go to synagogue, where we worship God. As part of our prayer service, the *ba'al tekiah* (the owner of the blast) blows the **shofar**, which is a ram's horn. It's very loud! It reminds us to think about what we've done wrong and to do better in the new year.

SHOFAR

At home, Mom serves sliced apple and a bowl of honey to dip it in, a symbol of the sweet year we hope for. We have challah bread, too, which is usually shaped like a braid, but for Rosh Hashanah it's round—a symbol of a complete year. Mom bakes raisins into it, and we make it extra sweet with more honey. There's also honey cake, flavored with orange juice, orange zest, and—you guessed it—honey!

In the afternoon we walk four blocks to the river and throw bread crumbs in the flowing water as a symbol of throwing off our sins. Over the next ten days, we think about the past year and say sorry for what we've done wrong.

Rosh Hashanah is celebrated by Jews all over the world in September or October every year.

Then comes the holiest day, *Yom Kippur*, when Mom and Dad fast for 25 hours. We spend time in synagogue asking God to forgive us for what we've done wrong. The **shofar** is blown to end Yom Kippur and we start the new year afresh.

CHALLAH

MID-AUTUMN FESTIVAL

Hello! I'm Tingting, and I live in a water town called Zhu Jia Jiao in the city of Shanghai, China. It's called a water town because several rivers run through and around it.

Every year, we celebrate the **Mid-Autumn Festival**. It's often called the Moon Festival, because it's held when the Moon is at its biggest and brightest. We give thanks for a good harvest, and we share the festival (especially the food!) with our family and friends.

JADE RABBIT

MOONCAKES

Everybody eats **mooncakes** at festival time! They're round, like the Moon, and made of pastry with fillings like fruit and nuts or sweet bean paste. My dad's a great baker, and we make mooncakes together. He has special molds to make patterned tops for them, and we give some away as gifts. During the festival we also eat hairy crabs and sweet cakes flavored with scented yellow osmanthus flowers.

Dad hangs lanterns from the trees in our courtyard, then we set mooncakes and fruit on a table outside. It's an offering to the goddess Chang'e, who drank a special potion that made her live forever. She flew to the Moon, and we believe she's still there, with the **Jade Rabbit** to keep her company. My granny knitted me a jade rabbit to keep me company.

This festival is celebrated every September or October in China and some other East and Southeast Asian countries, and in many other parts of the world.

When we've admired the Moon, we walk around town. Lanterns hang everywhere, and we always see a huge dragon puppet dancing through the streets. I love to stand on a bridge, looking at the reflections in the water. A moon above me and a moon below!

KING'S DAY

Hello, I'm Lotte. I live with my family in Amsterdam in the Netherlands. On April 27, everybody in the country has a holiday to celebrate our king's birthday. It's called Koningsdag, and it's fantastic fun!

The king and queen visit different parts of the country each year. We saw them when they came to Amsterdam and shouted Gelukkige verjaardag! (Happy birthday!) to the king. I think he heard us!

GELUKKIGE VERJAARDAG!

King's Day is celebrated on April 27 in the Netherlands.

We wear our national color, orange, on King's Day. I have an orange top and orange jeans, and a curly orange wig. My brother Max wears a crazy orange hat and scarf. We see lots of silly, fun outfits when we go out. Our neighbor dresses his dog in a sweater and frilly skirt—orange, of course!

The streets are decorated with flags and orange bunting. Amsterdam has many canals, so it's not just the streets that are packed with people—the waterways are, too. We pass a lot of street parties and boat parties. There's music and dancing everywhere, with performers on street corners and in bars.

A King's Day treat is going to the flea markets, which spring up everywhere. Anyone can put down a blanket and lay out things to sell. There are even special places where kids can sell their toys, books, or clothes.

TOMPOUCE

Dad always buys us a pastry called **tompouce**. It's loaded with cream—really loaded. Usually they're topped with pink icing, but on King's Day they're orange. Mom likes taking a photo of us when we're halfway through a **tompouce** and an orange drink. Not a pretty sight!

CARNIVAL IN RIO

Olá from Brazil! I'm Miguel, and I live in Rio de Janeiro. Rio is famous for beautiful beaches and Carnival! The Rio Carnival is about 300 years old, and it takes over the whole city.

Every day hundreds of bands play in the streets, but the biggest event is a huge **samba** dancing parade.

Rio has many samba schools around the city. They don't teach samba dancing—they're clubs that compete to be the best in the parade. First they choose a theme. It might be from history, or a myth or a well-known book. Then, for a whole year, each school prepares, with thousands of musicians, dancers, choreographers, and designers.

At Carnival the mayor gives the city keys to **King Momo**. He's a jolly, mischievous man, and he sets the samba parade going! Before the floats come into view, the flag-bearer and "queen" of each school lead the dancers. They wear dazzling costumes decorated with sequins, feathers, beads, and glitter.

Carnival in Rio de Janeiro, Brazil, is celebrated in February or early March every year.

Then the floats appear, lit up in beautiful colors. The drivers and the engine are hidden inside, so they do seem to float along. I've seen a roaring dinosaur, a ship rolling on the waves, and an elephant waving its trunk and tossing its head. Drums beat out the samba rhythm, and it makes me want to dance. It's the most colorful, exciting parade ever!

You don't have to watch the parade to enjoy Carnival. There are concerts, street parties, and costume balls all over the city. Something for everyone—and samba, samba, samba everywhere!

COME DANCE WITH ME!

INDEX